MONSTERS OF THE ANIMAL KINGDOM

ANACONDAS

Rachel Lynette

PowerKiDS press

New York

For Claire

Published in 2013 by The Rosen Publishing Group, Inc.
29 East 21st Street, New York, NY 10010

First Edition

Editor: Jennifer Way
Book Design: Greg Tucker

Photo Credits: Cover James Gerholdt/Peter Arnold/Getty Images; p. 4 Ryan M. Bolton/Shutterstock.com; p. 5 Zvonimir Orec/Shutterstock.com; p. 6 David Persson/Shutterstock.com; p. 7 Peter Wollinga/Shutterstock.com; pp. 8–9 AlessandroZocc/Shutterstock.com; p. 10 Tier Und Naturfotografie J und C Sohns/Workbook Stock/Getty Images; p. 11 © H. Brehm/age fotostock; pp. 12–13 Wayne Lynch/All Canada Photos/Getty Images; p. 14 Tom Brakefield/Stockbyte/Thinkstock; pp. 15, 19 © Morales/age fotostock; p. 16 Joel Sartore/National Geographic/Getty Images; p. 17 Dr. Morley Read/Shutterstock.com; p. 18 Fotomiro/Shutterstock.com; p. 20 Ed George/National Geographic/Getty Images; p. 21 Thiago Fernandes/Flickr Open/Getty Images; p. 22 © Nacho Calonge/age fotostock.

Library of Congress Cataloging-in-Publication Data

Lynette, Rachel.
  Anacondas / by Rachel Lynette. — 1st ed.
     p. cm. — (Monsters of the animal kingdom)
  Includes index.
  ISBN 978-1-4488-9631-8 (library binding) — ISBN 978-1-4488-9719-3 (pbk.) —
  ISBN 978-1-4488-9726-1 (6-pack)
  1. Anaconda—Juvenile literature. I. Title.
  QL666.O63L96 2013
  597.96'7—dc23
                          2012017220

Manufactured in the United States of America

CPSIA Compliance Information: Batch #W13PK5: For Further Information contact Rosen Publishing, New York, New York at 1-800-237-9932

CONTENTS

ESOME ANACONDAS

ou saw an anaconda in the wild, would you
raid? Anacondas are big, but they are not
omous. Rather than killing their **prey** with
m, anacondas use their powerful bodies to
strict, or squeeze them to death.

naconda, shown here,
-yellow stripes down
of its head.

Like all snakes, anacondas are **reptiles**. Like all reptiles, they are **cold-blooded**, which means that their body temperatures are the same as their surroundings. Anacondas are part of a family of snakes that also includes boa constrictors and pythons. There are four **species** of anacondas. This book will focus on the green anaconda because it is the biggest and the most common.

In the wild, anacondas can be found only in South America. They live in the tropical rain forests of the Amazon and Orinoco river basins. They also live on the island of Trinidad.

naconda, as shown
, can almost disappear
e water. Anacondas are
ays close to water.

This Amazonian rain forest is the kind of habitat in which anacondas are found.

Anacondas spend most of their time in the water. In fact, they are sometimes called water boas. They like the shallow, muddy waters of marshes, swamps, and slow-moving streams. Anacondas can move quickly and quietly in the water. They are much slower when moving on land. When they are not in the water, anacondas sometimes hang out in nearby trees, basking in the sun.

A SIZABLE SNAKE

The green anaconda is the biggest snake in the world! The reticulated python can grow a little longer than the green anaconda, but the green anaconda is much thicker and heavier. Female green anacondas can grow to be more than 29 feet (9 m) long. They can weigh more than 550 pounds (249 kg). Female anacondas are much larger than males. Anacondas never stop growing. They get bigger and bigger each year.

An anaconda's body is covered in scales. Its olive green coloring and double row of dark spots help the snake blend into its surroundings.

Anacondas can be as thick as an adult person's waist!

SUPER SWIMMERS

An anaconda's body is perfectly suited for its life in the water. Its eyes and nostrils are on top of its head so that it can breathe and watch for prey while its body stays hidden underwater. Anacondas are excellent swimmers. They can swim underwater or on the surface.

All species of anacondas are good swimmers and live in habitats close to water.

Here you can see an anaconda feeding on an egret, a kind of bird, in Brazil.

An anaconda can also hold its breath and stay underwater for 10 minutes at a time!

An anaconda has a strong body for constricting its prey. Its body can also stretch and change shape in order to hold whatever size animal it swallows.

SCARY FACTS

1 Anacondas always swallow their food headfirst. That way the animal's legs fold neatly under its body, making it easier to swallow.

2 Most anacondas live for about 10 years.

3 Anacondas have been known to eat jaguars.

4 Anaconda babies come from eggs, but they hatch while they are still inside the mother's body.

5 Adult anacondas will sometimes eat baby anacondas, even their own!

6 An anaconda has nearly 100 small, sharp teeth that are curved backward in order to hold its prey in place.

7 A 1997 movie called *Anaconda*, starring Jennifer Lopez, was about a film crew that is kidnapped and forced to search for a giant anaconda.

8 During **mating** season, several male anacondas may form a ball around one female, called a breeding ball. They will stay this way for up to a month.

13

SQUEEZED TO DEATH

Anacondas are **carnivores**. They eat wild pigs, deer, birds, turtles, **caimans**, and large rodents called capybaras.

Anacondas do not stalk their prey. Instead, they wait quietly in the water for their prey to come to them. When an animal is within striking range,

Anacondas typically hunt at night to blend into the surroundings even more.

Here you can see the inside of a yellow anaconda's mouth. The small teeth in its jaw are used to grab its prey.

the anaconda will spring out of the water and grab the animal with its teeth. Then it will coil its body around the animal several times and squeeze until the animal can no longer breathe. Often, the anaconda pulls the animal underwater and it drowns before it is squeezed to death.

DEVOURING ITS PREY

Anacondas do not chew their food. Instead, they swallow the animal whole! The top and bottom parts of an anaconda's jaws are connected with stretchy **ligaments**. These ligaments stretch like rubber bands so the anaconda can open its mouth very wide. It can take several hours for an anaconda to swallow a large animal.

Here a bird has just been captured by an anaconda and is still trying to free itself from the snake's grip.

Although anacondas can go weeks without eating, to reach their maximum size, they have to eat more often.

Once an anaconda has eaten, it will need to rest in order to **digest** the food. Strong **acids** in the anaconda's stomach slowly digest the animal inside its body. The anaconda will not need to eat again for several weeks or even months!

Female anacondas have babies once a year in the spring. Several male anacondas may fight to mate with one female. An anaconda's pregnancy lasts six months. Anaconda mothers usually give birth to 20 to 40 babies at a time. Newborn anacondas are about 2 feet (61 cm) long.

The anaconda's forked tongue helps it sense what direction a smell is coming from. Males use their tongues to sense the presence of a female with which they can mate.

Here a group of male anacondas have formed a breeding ball around a female with which they want to mate.

Mother anacondas do not care for their babies at all. Within a couple hours of being born, baby anacondas can take care of themselves. They can swim and hunt. Baby anacondas prey on smaller animals such as frogs, rodents, fish, and birds. Anacondas grow quickly and can begin

ANACONDA PREDATORS

Adult anacondas are so large and deadly that they have few natural **predators**. The only animals that ever attack anacondas are jaguars and large caimans. Humans sometimes illegally hunt anacondas for their skins. They may also be hunted and sold to zoos or even used as pets!

This South American caiman caught a young anaconda and is eating it.

The caracara, shown here, is one of the many birds of prey that may hunt baby anacondas.

While adult anacondas do not have to worry much about predators, this is not true for baby anacondas. Because they are so small, they make an easy meal for many predators, including birds, jaguars, and other snakes. About half of all baby anacondas will be eaten

ANACONDAS AND PEOPLE

Even though there are no known incidences of an anaconda killing a human, most people are still afraid of them. Hunting anacondas is illegal in most countries. However, people who live in the Amazon sometimes kill anacondas illegally out of fear of them.

Fortunately, anacondas are not endangered at this time. Groups such as the Wildlife Conservation Society are studying anacondas in the wild to learn more about them.

Some people like to keep anacondas as pets!

GLOSSARY

acids (A-sudz) Things that break down matter faster than water does.

caimans (KAY-menz) Alligator-like animals that live in Central and South America.

carnivores (KAHR-neh-vorz) Animals that eat only other animals.

cold-blooded (KOHLD-bluh-did) Having body heat that changes with the heat around the body.

constrict (kun-STRIKT) To squeeze.

digest (dy-JEST) To break down food so that the body can use it.

ligaments (LIH-guh-ments) Tissues in the body that join bones to other bones.

mating (MAYT-ing) Coming together to make babies.

predators (PREH-duh-terz) Animals that kill other animals for food.

prey (PRAY) An animal that is hunted by another animal for food.

reptiles (REP-tylz) Cold-blooded animals with thin, dry pieces of skin called scales.

species (SPEE-sheez) One kind of living thing. All people are one species.

venomous (VEH-nuh-mis) Having a poisonous bite.

INDEX

WEBSITES

Due to the changing nature of Internet links, PowerKids Press has developed an online list of websites related to the subject of this book. This site is updated regularly. Please use this link to access the list: www.powerkidslinks.com/mak/anaco/